To

From

CW00404218

Let there be Joy

Panographs® by Ken Duncan

INTRODUCTION

Laughter is the greatest medicine and a merry heart brings healing to the whole body. How true this is. But in a busy world which is changing so rapidly it can be difficult to push aside the pressures of life. As you reflect upon the beauty of God's creation in these photographs, may the inspired wisdom of the accompanying text help lift you higher into the awesome sunshine of God's presence where joy abounds. Remember ... he who laughs, lasts.

Ken Duncan.

A friendly smile
makes you happy,
and good news
makes you feel strong.

You are
my strong shield,

and I trust you
completely.

You have helped me,
and I will celebrate
and thank you
in song.

The LORD's
instruction is right;
it makes
our hearts glad.

His Commands
shine brightly,
and they give us light.

I pray that God,
who gives hope,
will bless you with
complete happiness
and peace
because of your faith.

And may the power
of the Holy Spirit
fill you with hope.

Let all who run
to you for protection
always sing
joyful songs.

Provide shelter
for those who truly
love you
and let them rejoice.

Our LORD, you bless
those who live right,
and you shield them
with your kindness.

When I felt
my feet slipping,
you came
with your love
and kept me steady.

And when
I was burdened
with worries,
you comforted me
and made me
feel secure.

You have shown me
the path to life

and you make me
glad by being
near to me.

Sitting at
your right side,
I will always
be joyful.

A friendly smile makes you happy, and good news makes you feel strong.

PROVERBS 15:30

You are my strong shield, and I trust you completely. You have helped me, and I will celebrate and thank you in song.

PSALMS 28:7

The LORD's instruction is right; it makes our hearts glad. His commands shine brightly, and they give us light.

PSALMS 19:8

I pray that God, who gives hope, will bless you with complete happiness and peace because of your faith. And may the power of the Holy Spirit fill you with hope.

ROMANS 15:13

Let all who run to you for protection always sing joyful songs. Provide shelter for those who truly love you and let them rejoice. Our LORD, you bless those who live right, and you shield them with your kindness.

PSALMS 5:11

When I felt my feet slipping, you came with your love and kept me steady.
And when I was burdened with worries, you comforted me and made me feel secure.

PSALMS 94:18-19

You have shown me the path to life, and you make me glad by being near to me. Sitting at your right side, I will always be joyful.

PSALMS 16:11

PHOTO INDEX

Let there be Joy

LET THERE BE JOY
FIRST PUBLISHED IN 1997
BY KEN DUNCAN PANOGRAPHS® PTY LTD
ACN 050 235 606
PO BOX 15, WAMBERAL NSW 2260
TELEPHONE: (02) 4367 6777

ISBN 0 9586681 5 9
PHOTOGRAPHY© KEN DUNCAN 1997
CEV TEXT© AMERICAN BIBLE SOCIETY 1995

DISTRIBUTED BY
THE BIBLE SOCIETY IN AUSTRALIA INC.
30 YORK ROAD, INGLEBURN NSW 2565
PRINTED IN HONG KONG BY SOUTH
CHINA PRINTING CO.